This journal belongs to: _____

Date: _____

If found, email/call: _____

Exploring Paths™ Daily Two-Minute Morning Gratitude Journal!

30-Day Challenge

Del Rio, TX Edition

Katherine Elizabeth Long

The publisher and the author make no guarantees concerning the level of success you may experience by following the advice and strategies container in this book, and you accept the risk that results will differ for each individual. Testimonials provided are not intended to represent or guarantee that you will achieve the same or similar results.

Also, this book does not replace the advice of a medical professional.
If you or someone you know is experiencing suicidal thoughts or crisis, please reach out to the Suicide Prevention Lifeline at 800-273-8255 or text HOME to the Crisis Text Line at 741741.
These services are free and confidential.

Exploring Paths™
Publishing

www.exploringpathspublishing.com

Printed by Exploring Paths™ Publishing, in the United States of America.

First printing, 2023.

Exploring Paths™ Publishing
12 Gay Road #1306
East Hampton, NY 11937

To the students of Del Rio, dream big, dare to be different, work hard, spread joy, and always pay things forward. Growing up in Del Rio is an advantage, whether you stay or set out to other destinations. I am grateful for each of you, as I know our world will be better because of you and all that you're learning in our hometown. I am excited to see what you create!

Thank You to **The Khoury Group** for helping make this partnership and work possible.

To **Del Rio Cares,** we're excited to support your efforts.

To **My Parents**, and especially to **My Dad**, I love you always. Your love of (and lessons to) James and me are the basis of this journal. And your passion, service, and dedication to Del Rio live on through this and us.

May this work help light the paths to all of your dreams and purpose and spread a little joy along the way. From one Del Rioan to another, thank you, and know that my team and I are cheering each of you on!
- Katherine

INTRODUCTION

Did you know that Gratitude has the power to physically change your brain and the way you think, act, and feel for the better? Scientists have studied it for years, and it does! When we practice Gratitude, our brains physically change, leading us to be happier, healthier, and more focused on solutions. This, in turn, helps us boost our creativity, set goals and achieve them, and build stronger relationships with friends, family, and teachers.

Welcome to your very own Exploring Paths® Daily Two-Minute Gratitude Journal 30-Day Challenge For Kids - Del Rio, TX Edition! We are excited to have you with us learning and feeling the power of Gratitude.

Gratitude is both saying thank you and, more importantly, *feeling* thankful and happy for something big or small and wanting to share kindness in return. The feeling of joy and happiness is what makes us smile when we receive or see something we truly like or spend time with people or in places we love. When we experience these feelings, don't we instantly want to say "thank you" to whoever or whatever gave them to us? Of course! That is Gratitude. It's not only saying thank you; it's feeling it and meaning it.

Gratitude works to change our brains and us for the better because our brains need those feelings in order to see and look for the good around us. Just like moving is good for our bodies, Gratitude is good for our minds. When we choose to focus on the good, we are training or exercising our brains to see the good and seek more of it automatically. Seeing and looking for the good is what helps us solve puzzles, feel happy, work towards our goals, and more.

Our workbooks inspire you to become more creative, set goals and achieve them, find joy, and boost your success at school and home through the practice of Gratitude. They are fun and straightforward and use repetition to develop the habit and practice of Gratitude.

GETTING STARTED

Are you ready to make your brain and mind stronger and feel happier and healthier? Just like with sports, music, riding a bicycle, and playing video games, practice makes perfect. So let's get started!

First, fill out your "About Me" section and create a vision board with your goals and what you want to have. We must see our goals and dreams in order to make them happen.

Next, take a few minutes each morning to think about your favorite memories from the day before, acknowledge how you're feeling, and then think about what you're grateful for, your goals, and who or what you want to thank. You will also think about simple acts of kindness you'd like to do during the day and imagine how you want your day to go.

If you need inspiration, write down what makes you smile when you see, feel, or hear it. Maybe it's being outside, a favorite teacher, or a smile from a friend. Perhaps it's your favorite food or a parent or parental figure. Start with the basics!

It's also important to know that having moments of not feeling okay is normal. It's our body telling us something is wrong. Crying or taking a walk or a quiet moment is good way to let out the bad, and then when you are ready, this workbook is here to share tools to help you feel better. Please always speak to a trusted adult if you feel sad, upset, or need help.

Keep your workbook safe and express yourself in any way that makes you smile. Be as specific as possible with your gratitudes, goals, and visions. And if you want to add some extra fun, take a few minutes to share your gratitude out loud and spread the kindness and joy.

When we practice gratitude and kindness, we open ourselves up to even more of it. Let's be grateful together and show the world what we can do!

We're grateful for you and your smile, so let's get started!

_____

(My name is)

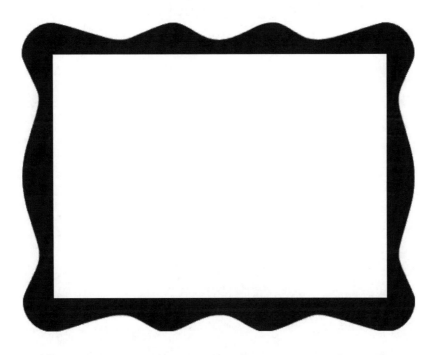

(My picture or my own self portrait is abovel)

ABOUT ME

(I will write a few sentences below about what makes me me.)

_____

_____

_____

_____

_____

_____

MY VISION BOARD

Vision boards are a collage of images and words that show a person's wishes or goals. They help inspire or motivate us to work towards what we want. (I will use this space to create my own vision board, and will write, draw, or attach pictures that reflect items, phrases, and goals I have.)

MY VISION BOARD CONTINUED

Staying positive and grateful helps me succeed, and I'm ready to get started!

DAY 1

Today is: _____

I'm feeling: Excited Happy Okay Sad Upset and/or _____

Today I am so happy & grateful for (be specific!):

1. _____
2. _____
3. _____

What made me smile yesterday:

1. _____
2. _____
3. _____

Today's goals:

1. _____
2. _____
3. _____

Acts of kindness to do today:

1. _____
2. _____
3. _____

People I want to thank:

1. _____
2. _____
3. _____

My vision for today is...
(I will write or draw how I see my day ahead and say Thank You when done).

DAY 2

Today is: _____

I'm feeling: Excited Happy Okay Sad Upset and/or _____

Today I am so happy & grateful for (be specific!):

1. _____
2. _____
3. _____

What made me smile yesterday:

1. _____
2. _____
3. _____

Today's goals:

1. _____
2. _____
3. _____

Acts of kindness to do today:

1. _____
2. _____
3. _____

People I want to thank:

1. _____
2. _____
3. _____

My vision for today is...
(I will write or draw how I see my day ahead and say Thank You when done).

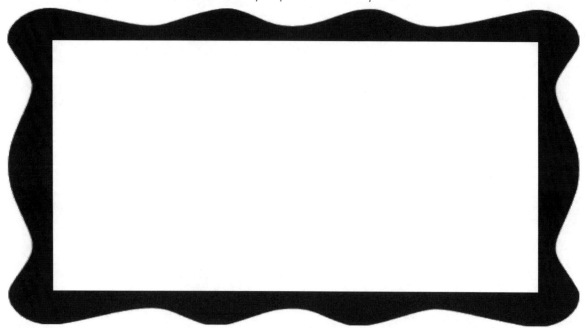

DAY 3

Today is: _____

I'm feeling: Excited Happy Okay Sad Upset and/or _____

Today I am so happy & grateful for (be specific!):

1. _____
2. _____
3. _____

What made me smile yesterday:

1. _____
2. _____
3. _____

Today's goals:

1. _____
2. _____
3. _____

Acts of kindness to do today:

1. _____
2. _____
3. _____

People I want to thank:

1. _____
2. _____
3. _____

My vision for today is...
(I will write or draw how I see my day ahead and say Thank You when done).

9

DAY 4

Today is: _____

I'm feeling: Excited Happy Okay Sad Upset and/or _____

Today I am so happy & grateful for (be specific!):

1. _____
2. _____
3. _____

What made me smile yesterday:

1. _____
2. _____
3. _____

Today's goals:

1. _____
2. _____
3. _____

Acts of kindness to do today:

1. _____
2. _____
3. _____

People I want to thank:

1. _____
2. _____
3. _____

My vision for today is...
(I will write or draw how I see my day ahead and say Thank You when done).

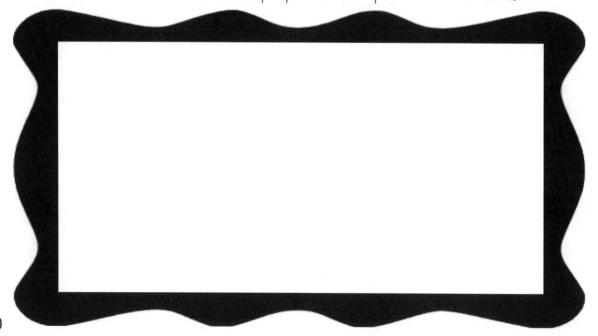

DAY 5

Today is: _____

I'm feeling: Excited Happy Okay Sad Upset and/or _____

Today I am so happy & grateful for (be specific!):

1. _____
2. _____
3. _____

What made me smile yesterday:

1. _____
2. _____
3. _____

Today's goals:

1. _____
2. _____
3. _____

Acts of kindness to do today:

1. _____
2. _____
3. _____

People I want to thank:

1. _____
2. _____
3. _____

My vision for today is...
(I will write or draw how I see my day ahead and say Thank You when done).

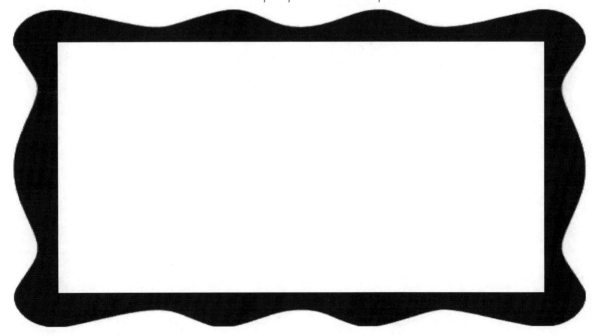

DAY 6

Today is: _____

I'm feeling: Excited Happy Okay Sad Upset and/or _____

Today I am so happy & grateful for (be specific!):

1. _____
2. _____
3. _____

What made me smile yesterday:

1. _____
2. _____
3. _____

Today's goals:

1. _____
2. _____
3. _____

Acts of kindness to do today:

1. _____
2. _____
3. _____

People I want to thank:

1. _____
2. _____
3. _____

My vision for today is...
(I will write or draw how I see my day ahead and say Thank You when done).

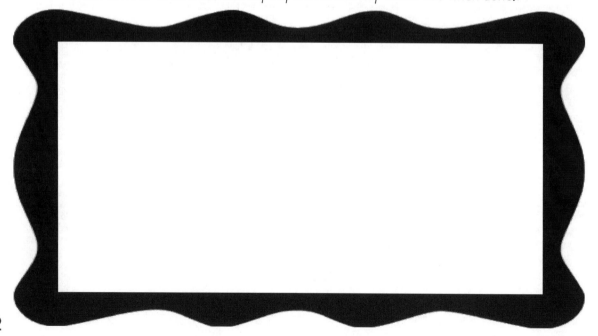

FIRST SIX WEEKS IS DONE!

Congrats, you finished week six of your 30-Day Gratitude Challenge!

How did it go? Draw or write about the following: How do I feel? What have I learned? What did I finish? What feelings and habits do I want to keep? What excites me? Be as descriptive as possible.

NOTES, POSITIVE THOUGHTS, REFLECTIONS

(I will use this space to write or draw any additional thoughts or feelings I have, and will remember to focus on the good I want to happen or do.)

I believe in myself
completely and have all
the tools I need to
succeed.

DAY 7

Today is: _____

I'm feeling: Excited Happy Okay Sad Upset and/or _____

Today I am so happy & grateful for (be specific!):

1. _____
2. _____
3. _____

What made me smile yesterday:

1. _____
2. _____
3. _____

Today's goals:

1. _____
2. _____
3. _____

Acts of kindness to do today:

1. _____
2. _____
3. _____

People I want to thank:

1. _____
2. _____
3. _____

My vision for today is...
(I will write or draw how I see my day ahead and say Thank You when done).

16

DAY 8

Today is: _____

I'm feeling: Excited Happy Okay Sad Upset and/or _____

Today I am so happy & grateful for (be specific!):

1. _____
2. _____
3. _____

What made me smile yesterday:

1. _____
2. _____
3. _____

Today's goals:

1. _____
2. _____
3. _____

Acts of kindness to do today:

1. _____
2. _____
3. _____

People I want to thank:

1. _____
2. _____
3. _____

My vision for today is...
(I will write or draw how I see my day ahead and say Thank You when done).

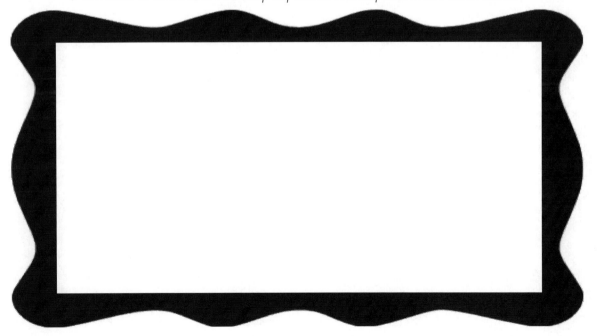

17

DAY 9

Today is: _____

I'm feeling: Excited Happy Okay Sad Upset and/or _____

Today I am so happy & grateful for (be specific!):

1. _____
2. _____
3. _____

What made me smile yesterday:

1. _____
2. _____
3. _____

Today's goals:

1. _____
2. _____
3. _____

Acts of kindness to do today:

1. _____
2. _____
3. _____

People I want to thank:

1. _____
2. _____
3. _____

My vision for today is...
(I will write or draw how I see my day ahead and say Thank You when done).

18

DAY 10

Today is: _____

I'm feeling: Excited Happy Okay Sad Upset and/or _____

Today I am so happy & grateful for (be specific!):

1. _____
2. _____
3. _____

What made me smile yesterday:

1. _____
2. _____
3. _____

Today's goals:

1. _____
2. _____
3. _____

Acts of kindness to do today:

1. _____
2. _____
3. _____

People I want to thank:

1. _____
2. _____
3. _____

My vision for today is...
(I will write or draw how I see my day ahead and say Thank You when done).

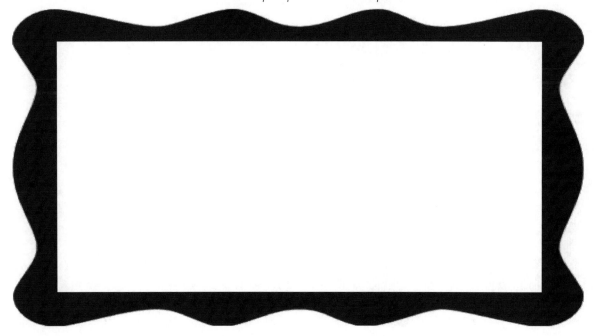

DAY 11

Today is: _____

I'm feeling: Excited Happy Okay Sad Upset and/or _____

Today I am so happy & grateful for (be specific!):

1. _____
2. _____
3. _____

What made me smile yesterday:

1. _____
2. _____
3. _____

Today's goals:

1. _____
2. _____
3. _____

Acts of kindness to do today:

1. _____
2. _____
3. _____

People I want to thank:

1. _____
2. _____
3. _____

My vision for today is...
(I will write or draw how I see my day ahead and say Thank You when done).

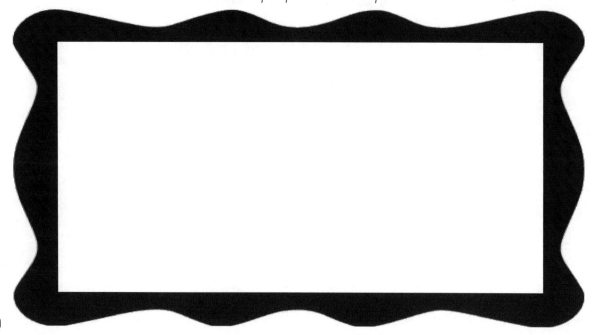

DAY 12

Today is: _____

I'm feeling: Excited Happy Okay Sad Upset and/or _____

Today I am so happy & grateful for (be specific!):

1. _____
2. _____
3. _____

What made me smile yesterday:

1. _____
2. _____
3. _____

Today's goals:

1. _____
2. _____
3. _____

Acts of kindness to do today:

1. _____
2. _____
3. _____

People I want to thank:

1. _____
2. _____
3. _____

My vision for today is...

(I will write or draw how I see my day ahead and say Thank You when done).

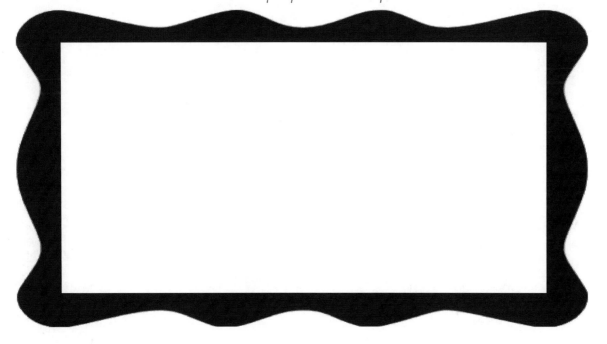

21

SIX WEEKS #TWO IS THROUGH!

Look at you go! You're halfway there, only two more 6-week periods!

Draw or write about the following: How do I feel? What have I learned? What did I finish? What feelings and habits do I want to keep? What excites me? Be as descriptive as possible.

NOTES, POSITIVE THOUGHTS, REFLECTIONS

(I will use this space to write or draw any additional thoughts or feelings I have, and will remember to also focus on the good I want to happen or do.)

My optimistic and grateful mindset attracts positive outcomes for which I am thankful.

DAY 13

Today is: _____

I'm feeling: Excited Happy Okay Sad Upset and/or _____

Today I am so happy & grateful for (be specific!):

1. _____
2. _____
3. _____

What made me smile yesterday:

1. _____
2. _____
3. _____

Today's goals:

1. _____
2. _____
3. _____

Acts of kindness to do today:

1. _____
2. _____
3. _____

People I want to thank:

1. _____
2. _____
3. _____

My vision for today is...
(I will write or draw how I see my day ahead and say Thank You when done).

25

DAY 14

Today is: _____

I'm feeling: Excited Happy Okay Sad Upset and/or _____

Today I am so happy & grateful for (be specific!):

1. _____
2. _____
3. _____

What made me smile yesterday:

1. _____
2. _____
3. _____

Today's goals:

1. _____
2. _____
3. _____

Acts of kindness to do today:

1. _____
2. _____
3. _____

People I want to thank:

1. _____
2. _____
3. _____

My vision for today is...
(I will write or draw how I see my day ahead and say Thank You when done).

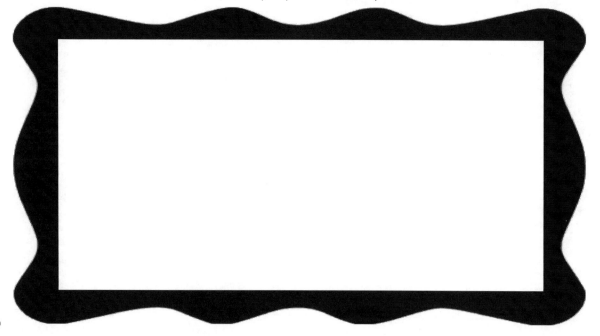

DAY 15

Today is: _____

I'm feeling: Excited Happy Okay Sad Upset and/or _____

Today I am so happy & grateful for (be specific!):

1. _____
2. _____
3. _____

What made me smile yesterday:

1. _____
2. _____
3. _____

Today's goals:

1. _____
2. _____
3. _____

Acts of kindness to do today:

1. _____
2. _____
3. _____

People I want to thank:

1. _____
2. _____
3. _____

My vision for today is...
(I will write or draw how I see my day ahead and say Thank You when done).

DAY 16

Today is: _____

I'm feeling: Excited Happy Okay Sad Upset and/or _____

Today I am so happy & grateful for (be specific!):

1. _____
2. _____
3. _____

What made me smile yesterday:

1. _____
2. _____
3. _____

Today's goals:

1. _____
2. _____
3. _____

Acts of kindness to do today:

1. _____
2. _____
3. _____

People I want to thank:

1. _____
2. _____
3. _____

My vision for today is...
(I will write or draw how I see my day ahead and say Thank You when done).

DAY 17

Today is: _____

I'm feeling: Excited Happy Okay Sad Upset and/or _____

Today I am so happy & grateful for (be specific!):

1. _____
2. _____
3. _____

What made me smile yesterday:

1. _____
2. _____
3. _____

Today's goals:

1. _____
2. _____
3. _____

Acts of kindness to do today:

1. _____
2. _____
3. _____

People I want to thank:

1. _____
2. _____
3. _____

My vision for today is...

(I will write or draw how I see my day ahead and say Thank You when done).

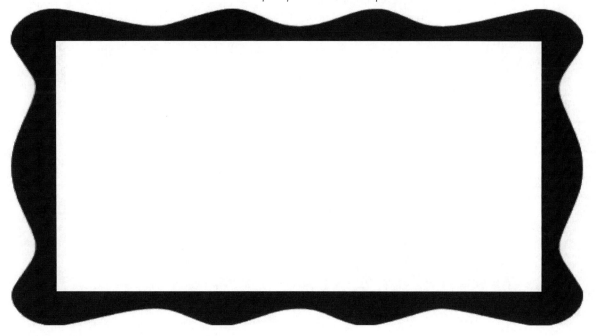

DAY 18

Today is: _____

I'm feeling: Excited Happy Okay Sad Upset and/or _____

Today I am so happy & grateful for (be specific!):

1. _____
2. _____
3. _____

What made me smile yesterday:

1. _____
2. _____
3. _____

Today's goals:

1. _____
2. _____
3. _____

Acts of kindness to do today:

1. _____
2. _____
3. _____

People I want to thank:

1. _____
2. _____
3. _____

My vision for today is...
(I will write or draw how I see my day ahead and say Thank You when done).

THIRD SIX WEEKS COMPLETE!

You're already a pro!

Draw or write about the following: How do I feel? What have I learned? What did I finish? What feelings and habits do I want to keep? What excites me? Be as descriptive as possible.

NOTES, POSITIVE THOUGHTS, REFLECTIONS

(I will use this space to write or draw any additional thoughts or feelings I have, and will remember to also focus on the good that I want to happen or do.)

I can make someone's day with a simple compliment or a smile.

DAY 19

Today is: _____

I'm feeling: Excited Happy Okay Sad Upset and/or _____

Today I am so happy & grateful for (be specific!):

1. _____
2. _____
3. _____

What made me smile yesterday:

1. _____
2. _____
3. _____

Today's goals:

1. _____
2. _____
3. _____

Acts of kindness to do today:

1. _____
2. _____
3. _____

People I want to thank:

1. _____
2. _____
3. _____

My vision for today is...
(I will write or draw how I see my day ahead and say Thank You when done).

DAY 20

Today is: _____

I'm feeling: Excited Happy Okay Sad Upset and/or _____

Today I am so happy & grateful for (be specific!):

1. _____
2. _____
3. _____

What made me smile yesterday:

1. _____
2. _____
3. _____

Today's goals:

1. _____
2. _____
3. _____

Acts of kindness to do today:

1. _____
2. _____
3. _____

People I want to thank:

1. _____
2. _____
3. _____

My vision for today is...
(I will write or draw how I see my day ahead and say Thank You when done).

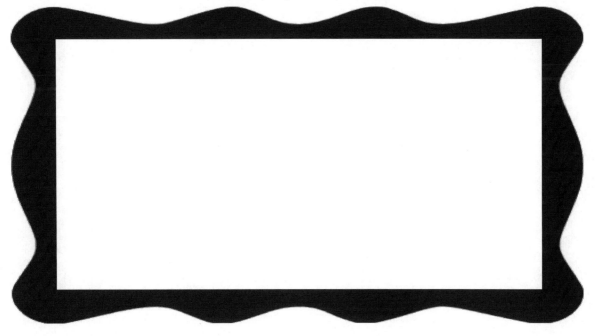

DAY 21

Today is: _____

I'm feeling: Excited Happy Okay Sad Upset and/or _____

Today I am so happy & grateful for (be specific!):

1. _____
2. _____
3. _____

What made me smile yesterday:

1. _____
2. _____
3. _____

Today's goals:

1. _____
2. _____
3. _____

Acts of kindness to do today:

1. _____
2. _____
3. _____

People I want to thank:

1. _____
2. _____
3. _____

My vision for today is...
(I will write or draw how I see my day ahead and say Thank You when done).

DAY 22

Today is: _____

I'm feeling: Excited Happy Okay Sad Upset and/or _____

Today I am so happy & grateful for (be specific!):

1. _____
2. _____
3. _____

What made me smile yesterday:

1. _____
2. _____
3. _____

Today's goals:

1. _____
2. _____
3. _____

Acts of kindness to do today:

1. _____
2. _____
3. _____

People I want to thank:

1. _____
2. _____
3. _____

My vision for today is...
(I will write or draw how I see my day ahead and say Thank You when done).

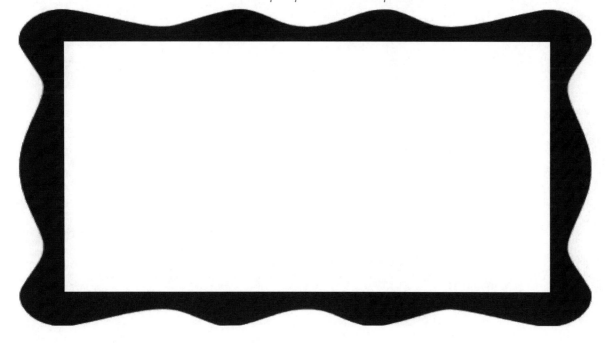

DAY 23   Today is: _____

I'm feeling: Excited Happy Okay Sad Upset and/or _____

Today I am so happy & grateful for (be specific!):

1. _____
2. _____
3. _____

What made me smile yesterday:

1. _____
2. _____
3. _____

Today's goals:

1. _____
2. _____
3. _____

Acts of kindness to do today:

1. _____
2. _____
3. _____

People I want to thank:

1. _____
2. _____
3. _____

My vision for today is...
(I will write or draw how I see my day ahead and say Thank You when done).

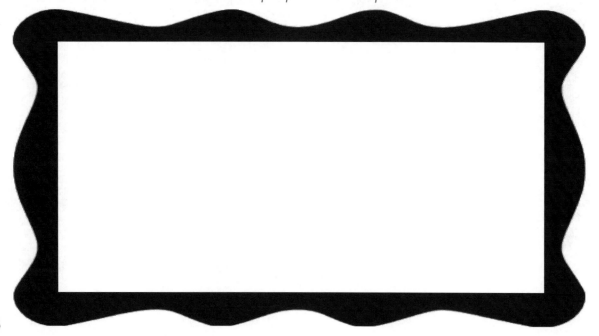

DAY 24

Today is: _____

I'm feeling: Excited Happy Okay Sad Upset and/or _____

Today I am so happy & grateful for (be specific!):

1. _____
2. _____
3. _____

What made me smile yesterday:

1. _____
2. _____
3. _____

Today's goals:

1. _____
2. _____
3. _____

Acts of kindness to do today:

1. _____
2. _____
3. _____

People I want to thank:

1. _____
2. _____
3. _____

My vision for today is...
(I will write or draw how I see my day ahead and say Thank You when done).

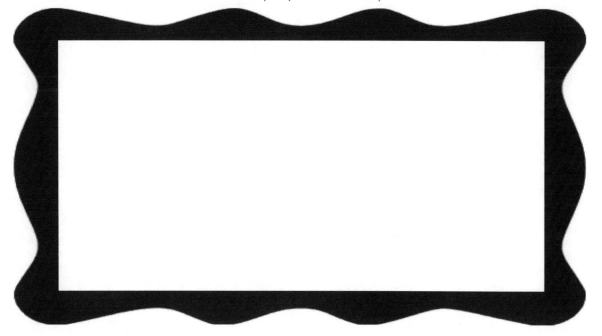

SIX WEEKS #FOUR!

You're nearly through that door!

Draw or write about the following: How do I feel? What have I learned? What did I finish? What feelings and habits do I want to keep? What excites me? Be as descriptive as possible.

NOTES, POSITIVE THOUGHTS, REFLECTIONS

(I will use this space to write or draw any additional thoughts or feelings I have, and will remember to also focus on the good I want to happen or do.)

I can accomplish what I put my mind, enthusiasm, and efforts toward.

DAY 25

Today is: _____

I'm feeling: Excited Happy Okay Sad Upset and/or _____

Today I am so happy & grateful for (be specific!):

1. _____
2. _____
3. _____

What made me smile yesterday:

1. _____
2. _____
3. _____

Today's goals:

1. _____
2. _____
3. _____

Acts of kindness to do today:

1. _____
2. _____
3. _____

People I want to thank:

1. _____
2. _____
3. _____

My vision for today is...

(I will write or draw how I see my day ahead and say Thank You when done).

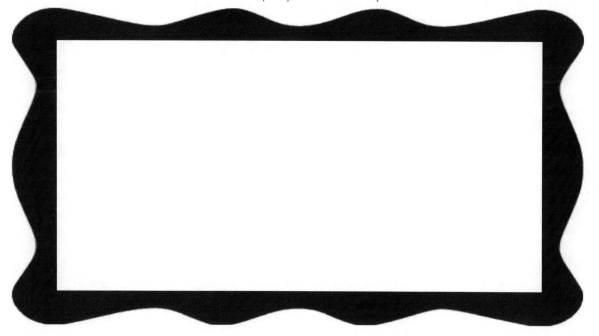

DAY 26

Today is: _____

I'm feeling: Excited Happy Okay Sad Upset and/or _____

Today I am so happy & grateful for (be specific!):

1. _____
2. _____
3. _____

What made me smile yesterday:

1. _____
2. _____
3. _____

Today's goals:

1. _____
2. _____
3. _____

Acts of kindness to do today:

1. _____
2. _____
3. _____

People I want to thank:

1. _____
2. _____
3. _____

My vision for today is...
(I will write or draw how I see my day ahead and say Thank You when done).

44

DAY 27

Today is: _____

I'm feeling: Excited Happy Okay Sad Upset and/or _____

Today I am so happy & grateful for (be specific!):

1. _____
2. _____
3. _____

What made me smile yesterday:

1. _____
2. _____
3. _____

Today's goals:

1. _____
2. _____
3. _____

Acts of kindness to do today:

1. _____
2. _____
3. _____

People I want to thank:

1. _____
2. _____
3. _____

My vision for today is...
(I will write or draw how I see my day ahead and say Thank You when done).

45

DAY 28

Today is: _____

I'm feeling: Excited Happy Okay Sad Upset and/or _____

Today I am so happy & grateful for (be specific!):

1. _____
2. _____
3. _____

What made me smile yesterday:

1. _____
2. _____
3. _____

Today's goals:

1. _____
2. _____
3. _____

Acts of kindness to do today:

1. _____
2. _____
3. _____

People I want to thank:

1. _____
2. _____
3. _____

My vision for today is...
(I will write or draw how I see my day ahead and say Thank You when done).

DAY 29   Today is: _____

I'm feeling: Excited Happy Okay Sad Upset and/or _____

Today I am so happy & grateful for (be specific!):

1. _____
2. _____
3. _____

What made me smile yesterday:

1. _____
2. _____
3. _____

Today's goals:

1. _____
2. _____
3. _____

Acts of kindness to do today:

1. _____
2. _____
3. _____

People I want to thank:

1. _____
2. _____
3. _____

My vision for today is...
(I will write or draw how I see my day ahead and say Thank You when done).

47

DAY 30

Today is: _____

I'm feeling: Excited Happy Okay Sad Upset and/or _____

Today I am so happy & grateful for (be specific!):

1. _____
2. _____
3. _____

What made me smile yesterday:

1. _____
2. _____
3. _____

Today's goals:

1. _____
2. _____
3. _____

Acts of kindness to do today:

1. _____
2. _____
3. _____

People I want to thank:

1. _____
2. _____
3. _____

My vision for today is...

(I will write or draw how I see my day ahead and say Thank You when done).

YOU DID IT!!

30 Days under your belt! An accomplishment you should be proud of!

I know what's next...:) Draw or write about the following: How do I feel? What have I learned? What did I finish? What feelings and habits do I want to keep? What excites me? Be as descriptive as possible.

MY VISION BOARD

Vision boards are a collage of images and words that show a person's wishes or goals. They help inspire or motivate us to work towards what we want. (I will use this space to create my own vision board, and will write, draw, or attach pictures that reflect items, phrases, and goals I have.)

MY VISION BOARD - CONTINUED

NOTES, POSITIVE THOUGHTS, REFLECTIONS

(I will use this space to write or draw any additional thoughts or feelings I have, and will remember to also focus on the good I want to happen or do.)

CONCLUSION

We are all here for a reason, to find our paths and to be the person we're supposed to become. Gratitude and goal-setting are the surefire way to catapult each of us onto that path.

We hope the past 30 days and this journal have helped you create a new morning ritual that brings you joy, learning, and a greater appreciation for each other and all that we have, big or small!

Gratitude, growth mindset, and goal-setting are the foundations for success and happiness in all aspects of our lives. While it can take anywhere from 18 to 66 days to form a new habit (sometimes longer), you are well on your way to having gratitude and goal-setting stick if it hasn't already!

Our goal was to provide the framework to practice gratitude daily and show you that a little can go a long way!

With gratitude and love, we're cheering you on!
Katherine & The Exploring Paths™ Publishing Team

Made in the USA
Middletown, DE
23 August 2024

59249066R00033